Caring for a Colony

The Story of Jeanne Mance

Caring for a Colony

The Story of Jeanne Mance

by

Joanna Emery

Illustrations by Chrissie Wysotski

Series Editor: Allister Thompson

Napoleon Publishing

Napoleon Publishing
Toronto Ontario Canada

Napoleon Publishing acknowledges
the support of the Canada Council for the Arts
for our publishing program.

Le Conseil des Arts | The Canada Council
du Canada | for the Arts

Printed in Canada

Library and Archives Canada Cataloguing in Publication

Emery, Joanna
Caring for a colony : the story of Jeanne Mance / Joanna Emery.

(Stories of Canada)
ISBN 1-894917-07-3

1. Mance, Jeanne, 1606-1673--Juvenile literature. 2. Hôtel-Dieu
de Montréal--History--Juvenile literature. 3. Nurses--Canada--Biography--
Juvenile literature. 4. Canada--History--To 1763 (New France)--Juvenile
literature. I. Title. II. Series: Stories of Canada (Toronto, Ont.)

FC306.M35E44 2005   j971.01'6'092
C2005-903466-1

I dedicate this book to
my husband, Greg.

Was It a Miracle?

This miniature painted on wood is the closest image we have to an authentic portrait of Jeanne Mance. In the mid-nineteenth century, Sister Paquette, a nun and archivist at Hôtel-Dieu in Montreal, wrote on the back the words "true portrait of Miss Mance before coming to Canada, 1638."

Jeanne cradled the urn in her lap. She closed her eyes and thought of her old friend, the founder of the St. Sulpice Order, abbé Jean-Jacques Olier. He had died the year before her arrival in Paris and before her accident back in New France. A slip on the ice had left Jeanne's right arm badly damaged and completely immobile for more than eighteen months.

"I ask only for strength in my duties," she prayed softly. Inside the urn was the preserved heart of Monsieur Olier. As her lips moved in silence, a warm sensation tingled throughout her arm. Jeanne could not believe it. Her withered arm looked the same, but the pain was gone! She could move it as well as before the injury.

Was it a miracle? Or was it simply mind over matter? Jeanne certainly believed it was a miracle. One thing is sure: Jeanne Mance had a strong will. Once she made a decision, nothing could stop her. She possessed an intense desire to serve and care for others. Her courage carried her across the ocean seven times. Her devotion made her the founder of Montreal's first hospital, and her resourcefulness saved the new settlement from near destruction.

Jeanne has rightly been called "The Mother of Montreal".

Caring...and Curiosity

Jeanne grew up in Langres, France, a medieval town in the province of Champagne.

Jeanne would have loved the barn kittens, just as this little girl does.

From an early age, Jeanne Mance was taught to care. Perhaps, as a young girl, she treated wounded birds or fussed over the latest litter of newborn barn kittens. These fragile but determined creatures may have reminded Jeanne of herself. She had never been in perfect health, but that did not stop her.

Like most females in seventeenth-century Europe, Jeanne knew that when she grew up, she would be expected to devote her life to others. She could marry and tend to a husband and children or join a religious order and become a nun. Many nuns taught or actively served the poor. Some were cloistered and remained secluded in convents. Their duty was to pray for the welfare of the world.

Jeanne had something else in common with those barn kittens, an intense curiosity. Outside her comfortable home was a world of adventure. For the kittens, this meant the fields and meadows. For Jeanne, her destiny lay five thousand miles away in a colony in North America called New France.

JACQUES CARTIER

Who discovered Canada? In 1534, Jacques Cartier claimed the land for France. But the discovery of a Norse settlement in today's Newfoundland proved that other Europeans had arrived at least as early as 992 A.D.

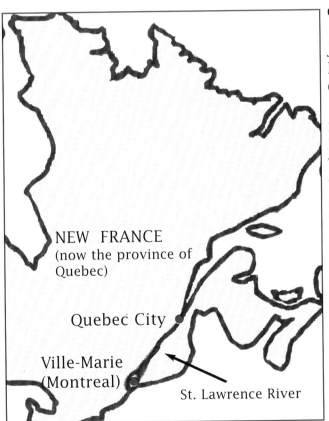

NEW FRANCE
(now the province of Quebec)

Quebec City

Ville-Marie
(Montreal)

St. Lawrence River

Bravery Required

The name "Canada" comes from "kanata"—an aboriginal word for "village". In 1608, the year Jeanne Mance turned two, the French explorer, Samuel de Champlain, founded a settlement on the shores of today's St. Lawrence River and called it New France.

Decades earlier, another explorer named Jacques Cartier had travelled up the St. Lawrence River to the site of present-day Quebec City.

Quebec means "where the river narrows", although at the time, the First Peoples called their village Stadacona. They greeted the Europeans warmly, but when Cartier continued on to the village of Hochelaga, the site known today as Montreal, he offended the Native chief, Donnacona. Cartier and his men also unintentionally brought disease. During the first winter, at least fifty Native people died from European illnesses they had never known before, such as smallpox (or purple fever) and flu.

At first, France didn't have much interest in the new colony. Imagine that you have decided to live on Mars. The comments from friends and family would probably be the same: You're crazy! It's dangerous! You'll get killed there! Most people thought the same about New France. But there were two main reasons why some took the risk. One was for God, and the other was for money.

Valuable Furs

BEAVERS

When the fur trade began, there were about ten million beavers in Canada. Between 1660-1760, twenty-five million beaver pelts were exported to France. By the middle of the nineteenth century, beavers were almost extinct.

An 18th century illustration of a beaver

The "tails" side on a five-cent coin shows one important reason for the interest in New France, the beaver. Beaver fur, in particular. Its valuable, soft underfur was made into fashionable hats, a popular item in Europe, especially in Jeanne's France. Canada was full of animals with luxurious furs. Along with beaver, demand for lynx, wolf, bear and other pelts skyrocketed.

Cardinal Richelieu, the representative of the powerful Roman Catholic Church and of the French King, Louis XIII, gave merchant companies a monopoly on the fur trade in New France, meaning that no one else could trade in furs there. One such company was the *Compagnie des Cent-Associés* (Company of One Hundred Associates). In return for its rights, the Company had to encourage colonial settlements and missionaries, who would convert the Natives to Catholicism.

The Company distributed land, or *seigneuries*, to influential colonists. These *seigneurs* allowed tenants, called *habitants*, to live and work on the land in return for a portion of what they produced. This social order, called the seigneurial system, continued in New France for the next 225 years.

The lucrative fur trade had made this new, wild country important. But Jeanne's interest in New France wasn't about wealth. She simply wanted to serve God and bring people to the Church.

A Special Vow

JESUITS

The Jesuits were an international order founded by Ignatius Loyola in 1534. They thought of themselves as "soldiers for Christ" and believed that the best way to convert the Natives was to learn their ways and educate them. They were called the "Black Robes" by the Native peoples.

Jeanne's deep religious beliefs came from her upbringing. As devout Roman Catholics, her parents actively supported charities and were familiar with Catholic missionaries.

Two orders, the Récollets and the Jesuits, were the first French missionaries in New France. They tried to convert the First Peoples —the Natives—to Christianity and promote Catholicism throughout the colony. Well-educated and disciplined, the Jesuits kept detailed accounts, called *Relations,* of their daily work. The *Relations* became immensely popular in France, and it's likely that Jeanne's household had the latest copies.

At the age of seven, Jeanne made a vow. She told her family that she wanted to dedicate her life to God. She had no desire to become a nun, but she wasn't eager to get married either. In some unknown way, she hoped to use her faith to help others.

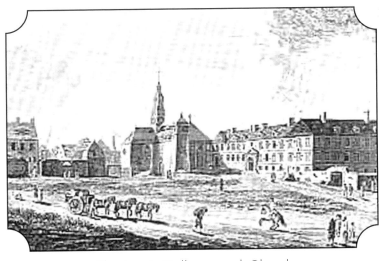

The Jesuit College and Church
in Quebec City in 1761

Schooling

THE MANCE CHILDREN

Marguerite (1605); Jeanne (1606); Marie (1608); Nicolas (1609); Jacques (1610); Barbe (1611); Pierre (1612); Claude (1614); Charles (1616); another Claude (1617); Elisabeth (1619); Catherine (1623).

CONVENTS

Since the early Middle Ages, religious women have lived in residences called convents. These usually housed nuns, but they were also often centres of learning with libraries and schools.

Not quite aristocratic nobles, the Mance family was part of the upper middle class, and still very privileged. As a prominent lawyer, Charles Mance made sure that all his children received an education. Jeanne and her older sister, Marguerite, were taught at the local Ursuline convent. The nuns showed the girls how to read, write and perform delicate arts such as embroidery. Jeanne probably learned about New France during her school years, but no one would have expected a well-bred lady like herself to ever travel to such a faraway place.

THE THIRTY YEARS' WAR

In 1618, a revolt by Protestants in Prague against the Catholic German states set off the Thirty Years War. The war was generally fought in the central European lands of the Holy Roman Empire but also involved Denmark, Sweden, England and later France. Peace finally came in 1648.

NOT-SO-MODERN MEDICINE

Hospitals in Jeanne's time were different from those of today. Nursing was hardly a respectable activity, and so-called doctors knew little about medicine. Their knowledge came from ancient texts and was based on the "four humours": blood, black bile, yellow bile and phlegm. A healthy body meant that these "humours" were in perfect balance. Cures to correct an imbalance included bloodletting (using leeches or cuts to remove "bad blood") and purging (such as making the patient vomit). Not surprisingly, few patients left these early hospitals alive.

Service

Jeanne didn't know it, but the coming years would test her childhood vow. As a teenager, she was frequently ill and never in the best health. When she was twenty, her mother died. Jeanne and Marguerite now had to help raise their ten younger siblings.

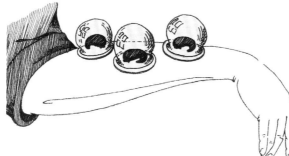

Bloodletting using leeches

In Langres, Jeanne saw her fellow country folk suffer major hardships, including a devastating plague and the Thirty Years' War. Jeanne, like many educated and devout French women, probably joined a charitable society to help the desperate and wounded soldiers. She quickly learned how to bandage wounds, apply compresses and tend to the patients' needs. In other words, Jeanne acted as a nurse.

In one year alone, 5,500 people in Jeanne's hometown perished from either war or plague. These trials simply made her determination, and her faith, stronger.

Jeanne's twenties were years of hard work and dedication to others.

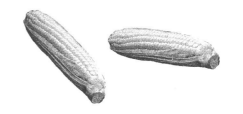

MADAME DE LA PELTRIE

Born three years before Jeanne Mance, Marie Madeleine de Chavigny married at the age of seventeen and became Madame de La Peltrie. Five years later, she was a widow. She too had read the Jesuit *Relations* and wanted to serve in Canada, but her late husband's relatives, and even her own father, were against it. But Madame de La Peltrie had a plan. She wrote to her friend, Monsieur de Bernières, and asked for his help. Would he agree to marry her? It was a chance to be free and go to New France. Monsieur de Bernières consented and they were married. Shortly after their "wedding", her father died, and, Madame de La Peltrie was free to travel to Quebec, where she established a hospital with the Ursuline Sisters and their superior, Marie de l'Incarnation.

An Exciting Visit

"Nicolas!" Jeanne stretched out her slender arms and embraced her cousin. "You've come to see me!" She had always been close to her relatives, but this visit was special. Nicolas Dolebeau, a priest and teacher, brought the latest news from Paris. His brother, John, was a Jesuit missionary in Canada.

Nicolas talked for hours about New France and the exciting missions leaving from the French port city of La Rochelle.

"A wealthy widow, Madame de La Peltrie, and several Ursuline nuns have already boarded ships bound for New France," he said. "They will assist the colonists and spread the Catholic faith."

The words struck Jeanne's heart like an arrow. Even though she was thirty-four years old, Jeanne knew this was a chance to fulfil her deepest desire and serve God. She desperately wanted to go.

A 17th century illustration of La Rochelle on the Atlantic coast

A Thoughtful Journey

Jeanne didn't doubt her longing to work in New France, but she felt uncertain about her motive. Like most Christians of her time, Jeanne abhorred sinfulness. Were her dreams realistic and, more important, genuinely unselfish? After consulting her parish priest, Jeanne was told to go to Paris and seek more guidance from the missionary priests there.

Keeping her true intentions secret, Jeanne left Langres for Paris. She had told her family that she was off to visit relatives. Since her father had died several years earlier, Jeanne's explanation didn't seem unusual. Perhaps they even hoped she'd return with a husband.

The journey took almost a month. In the jostling stagecoach, Jeanne thought deeply about her plans. Where would she find the money to travel across the ocean? Could she survive in New France, or even the dangerous voyage to get there? There were women there, such as Marie de l'Incarnation and the Ursulines. But was her faith and determination as strong as theirs?

Marie de l'Incarnation

Marie de l'Incarnation

Marie Guyart also dreamed of New France. She was born in 1599, the daughter of a master baker. Like most girls of her time, Marie married young, but her husband died when she was only nineteen. Since she had to raise her one-year-old son, Marie worked at managing the family silk business. Privately, she wore a prickly horsehair cloth under her clothes and had mystical religious visions. One recurring image was of her walking with another woman and founding a convent in a faraway place. When her son turned twelve, Marie sent him away to school, and she joined the Ursuline convent. The nuns were familiar with the Jesuit *Relations* and explained that her vision was of New France and the lady was Madame de La Peltrie.

Marie travelled to Quebec in 1639 and established the Ursuline convent and a school in what is now Quebec City. The many letters she wrote to her son back in France are a valuable record of her work.

Men and women who entered religious life often took new names. Marie changed hers to Marie de l'Incarnation when she became an Ursuline nun in 1631.

An aerial view of the convent and school of the Ursuline sisters in present-day Quebec City

SELF-DENIAL

As a penance for sins, the very religious were known to practice self-denial or voluntary punishments. Some would fast or wear coarse undershirts made of horse or goat hair while others went so far as to whip themselves and wear sharply pointed belts that cut the flesh.

SEDAN CHAIR

Jeanne often used a sedan chair when she visited Madame de Bullion. On one occasion, the chairmen who carried the sedan chair asked Jeanne why she weighed less coming than when she left, implying that she must have received many gifts. In fact, Madame de Bullion did give token presents, but Jeanne was so afraid of being robbed that she changed her visiting hours and even hired new chairmen!

MME DE BULLION

A street in Montreal is called Rue de Bullion and a wing of the Hôtel-Dieu Hospital is named "Pavillon de Bullion".

The Unknown Benefactress

The colony of New France would never have survived without contributions from the rich. When she heard that a French duchess had donated a large sum of money to fund the Hôtel-Dieu Hospital in Quebec, one aristocratic lady, Angélique Faure de Bullion, wanted to be equally generous. Her husband, a minister from Louis XIII's court, had recently died, and Madame de Bullion wished to use the money left her to build a hospital in the new settlement which would eventually be called Montreal.

Through her cousin Nicolas, Jeanne met influential people in the aristocratic society of Paris. One family friend, a priest named Charles Rapine, introduced Jeanne to Madame de Bullion. Quite impressed, the wealthy widow soon asked Jeanne to manage the project.

Jeanne was excited, but once again doubtful. Was she physically too frail for such a difficult task? Her adviser, the Jesuit Father Jean Baptiste Saint-Jure, told her not to worry, that "God wished her to go to Canada." After prayer and meditation, Jeanne was convinced. Her calling was in New France.

Jeanne was asked to make one important promise. Madame de Bullion believed that boasting about charity was a sin. She insisted that her name be kept secret. Through Father Rapine, Jeanne would inform Madame de Bullion of the hospital's progress. But no one was ever to know the identity of the "Unknown Benefactress".

City of God

MARIE DE LA FERRE

Marie de La Ferre (1592-1652), founder of the Congregation of the Daughters *Hospitalières* of Saint Joseph in 1636, known also as the Religious *Hospitalières* of St. Joseph (the RHSJ, or, in French, the *Religieuses Hospitalières de St-Joseph*.

Jérôme de La Dauversière, co-founder of the *Hospitalières*

SAVAGES

Europeans referred to the Native Peoples as "savages" because they thought Native ways were inferior to their own. In their attempt to civilize the Natives and convert them to the Christian religion, the Europeans actually destroyed many of the ancient Native traditions.

Jeanne pondered the advice she had received from Fathers Saint-Jure and Rapine: "Go to La Rochelle. Speak with La Dauversière."

Jérôme Le Royer de La Dauversière had rebuilt a hospital at La Flèche in France and, with Marie de La Ferre, founded the *Hospitalières de St-Joseph*. Married, with six children, La Dauversière had the reputation of being a mystic. He wore a belt of sharp points and whipped himself with small chains. He believed that God had told him to serve the Island of Montreal.

The abbé Jean-Jacques Olier heard the same voice. He established a group of priests, the Order of St. Sulpice, whose members would later serve in Ville-Marie, or Montreal. La Dauversière and Olier did not know each other, but they met by chance one day. It was destiny, they agreed. Thanks to the financial generosity of a wealthy Parisian, they founded the *Société de Notre-Dame de Montréal pour la conversion des sauvages* (Society of Our Lady of Montreal for the Conversion of the Savages).

WARS OF RELIGION

In the fifteenth century, attempts to reform the Catholic Church led to religious and social upheavals that eventually split Christendom. Struggles between Protestants and Catholics resulted in political conflicts and civil wars, the Wars of Religion, that raged throughout most of Europe for almost two hundred years.

The Society of Our Lady dreamed of making Ville-Marie a perfect Christian community. It was, in part, a response to the long European wars between Protestants and Catholics. Ville-Marie—as the Montreal settlement was called—would be served by three religious groups: one of priests to convert the Natives; one of nuns to nurse the sick; and another to teach the Catholic faith to the children. Each group was devoted to a member of the Holy Family—Jesus, Mary and Joseph. On a crisp February day, thirty-five members from the *Société de Notre-Dame de Montreal* attended a special mass at the Cathedral of Notre Dame in Paris. During the service, Father Olier officially dedicated Ville-Marie to the Holy Family. It was to become, as La Dauversière had envisioned, a true "City of God".

TEN POUNDS OF FISH

The Society of Our Lady acquired the Island of Montreal from Jean de Lauzon, Intendant of the Company of New France, for an annual rent of ten pounds of fish. They were now *seigneurs*, or the lords, of the Island of Montreal and could appoint a governor and establish courts.

Paul de Chomedy,
Sieur de Maisonneuve

Maisonneuve, like Jeanne, was a pious layperson. Trained as a soldier, one of his favourite pastimes was playing the lute. He is known as the first governor of Montreal. Despite incredible hardships and constant threat of Iroquois attack, he remained faithfully at his post for twenty-five years.

A Twist of Fate

Jeanne headed to the port town of La Rochelle, almost five hundred kilometres from Paris. As usual, she first attended Mass. Right outside the church, by strange coincidence, she met up with La Dauversière! They talked and he introduced her to the twenty-nine-year-old leader of the expedition to Ville-Marie, Paul de Chomedey, Sieur de Maisonneuve.

La Dauversière asked if Jeanne would join the Society as its eighth member and assured her that Maisonneuve would protect her as well as the new hospital. Would she accompany the expedition to New France, organize the household tasks, nurse the sick and help prepare the colony for the later arrival of the *Hospitalières*?

Jeanne hesitated. Once again she sought guidance and wrote to Father Saint-Jure and her cousin. Did they think she should go? They quickly replied: "Yes!"

Set to Sail

Before she left, Jeanne wrote to every influential person she knew in Paris requesting financial contributions for the Society. She gave the letters to La Dauversière and asked him to hand deliver each one. In return, the wealthy Parisians donated generously. Jeanne had become Montreal's first fundraiser,

Three ships made up the New France expedition, although one had already left from the French port of Dieppe. At La Rochelle, Maisonneuve and twenty-five colonists filled a second ship, while Jeanne boarded the third. Of the fourteen people on her ship, Jeanne was the only woman until, at the last minute, two sailors' wives and a young girl insisted on joining the expedition.

They set sail on the first day of June 1641. Jeanne stood on the windy deck and listened to the ship creak with each roll into the waves. Would they arrive safely? She watched a sailor pluck a chicken for that evening's dinner.

After the few livestock on board were eaten, the only food left was salt pork, hard biscuits, or, if they were lucky, a freshly-caught fish. When the ship's supply of fresh water ran out, rain would have to be collected from the sails. Going to the bathroom meant using a tin pail. Never in the best of health, the difficult journey made Jeanne very sick.

Arrival

FILTH

It was said of the Augustinian Sisters at the Hôtel-Dieu in Quebec that they worked so hard, in such filth, that they had to dye their white habits with butternut juice.

POSTAL SERVICE

Jeanne would have written by candlelight. She probably had no news of her family back in France during her stay in Quebec. Letters took a long time and depended on the ships. Sometimes, the same letter was written two or three times and sent on different ships to make sure at least one arrived at its destination.

New France, as the French called Quebec, had only a few hundred colonists when Jeanne first arrived. Virtually everyone rushed out to greet the vessel as it headed into port. Jeanne's ship was the first to reach the colony; Maisonneuve's had not yet arrived.

It didn't take long for Jeanne to meet Marie de l'Incarnation of the Ursuline Sisters. She had come to Quebec in 1639 with Madame de La Peltrie and three Sisters from the Augustine Order to establish the Hôtel-Dieu Hospital in Quebec.

The nuns led a strict and simple life, filled with prayer and service. Madame de La Peltrie, on the other hand, had not forgotten to bring over her expensive French furniture. As well as their devotion to God, Jeanne and the wealthy young widow had much in common and were soon to become good friends.

17

The First Peoples

An 18th century French illustration of an Iroquois warrior

THE IROQUOIS

The Iroquois Confederacy consisted of the Mohawk, Oneida, Onondaga, Cayuga and Seneca Nations. When the Tuscarora joined in the eighteenth century, they became known as the Six Nations—the "Haudenosaunee", which means "People of the Longhouse", because they lived in long lodges.

When Jeanne first saw the Native people, she was shocked. They were scantily clad in animal skins, and the men had a strange hairstyle. The French nicknamed them "hurons", which meant "ruffians".

Their real name was Wendat (also spelled Ouendat) and they, like other tribes of First Peoples, had lived in North America for thousands of years before the Europeans arrived. They introduced the colonists to new foods such as maize (corn), squash, wild rice and maple syrup, as well as tobacco. They did not believe anyone "owned" the land any more than one owned the rivers or the sky. Unfortunately, the fur trade made them more dependent on a European lifestyle. In time, most moved away from their traditional life.

Jeanne was told that the enemy was the Iroquois, a name given by the British, after a Native term that meant "black snakes". While traditional warfare existed between the different tribes before the Europeans arrived, the fur trade intensified the rivalries. Threatened with extinction, the Iroquois obtained weapons and iron goods from the Dutch and the British. Champlain, on the other hand, established French cooperation with tribes such as the Algonquin, Montagnais and Wendat. The result? Severe hostilities that were to last for generations to come.

BLACK ROBES

It was the usual practice to give guns to those Natives who accepted Catholicism. Therefore, some felt they had no choice but to accept the Jesuit missions. Not only did they depend on French firearms to fight the Iroquois' Dutch-made weapons, but they also thought that baptism might cure the new diseases such as smallpox. The "Black Robes", who performed magic ceremonies with their porcelain rosary beads, didn't seem to get smallpox. While some Natives accepted conversion, especially on their deathbeds, others blamed the Jesuits for war and disease.

Saving Souls

To the Europeans, Natives were "savages". They dressed, spoke and lived in a supposedly uncivilized manner. Even Jeanne used the term in her writings. She, like the Jesuits, thought that religious conversion would save their souls.

But the Native peoples already knew about the Creator, the Great Spirit. They deeply respected the earth—the Great Mother—and believed that everything in nature, including the animals, rocks and trees, had a spirit. Before the Europeans arrived, trade among their tribes was never for profit. They knew it was important to leave the land and its riches for those not yet born.

The Jesuit *Relations* tells that the Native elders enjoyed hearing the Jesuits preach, but "when urged to adopt the faith which so readily met with their approval, they had always the same reply: 'It is good for the French; but we are another people with different customs.'"

Ursuline sisters with Native children

A Foolish Venture?

COUREURS DES BOIS

The *coureurs des bois* (literally, "runners of the woods") were unlicensed fur traders in New France. In search of valuable furs, they ventured far into the wilderness and often grew accustomed to the Native way of life. While their activities helped in the expansion of New France, the government considered the *coureurs* a problem since they rarely settled down and usually sold liquor to the Natives.

The Quebec colonists called the Montreal expedition *la folle entreprise*—the foolish venture. Jealous that the ship's supplies were not for them, and in desperate need of Jeanne's nursing skills, they begged her to stay. "Why face unknown danger and inevitable Iroquois attacks?" they asked. But Jeanne stood her ground.

For nearly three weeks, she patiently waited for Maisonneuve's ship. During that time, Jeanne had much to discover in this New World. She saw what the colonists had learned from the First Peoples, such as how to make moccasins, toboggans, popcorn and maple syrup. She watched the *voyageurs* as they traded iron tools, tin pots and glass beads for heaps of fur pelts. She noticed the *coureurs des bois*—literally, the runners of the woods—Europeans who lived and dressed like First Peoples and could repair their snowshoes or cedar canoes with the greatest skill.

Winter Wait

CLOTHING

Ladies wore bonnets and men woollen caps with a fur or wool tassel on the tip. These were called "tuques", from the old French word "touche", meaning a small wooded hill.

With winter coming, the expedition party headed to Sillery, land near Quebec town given to the Jesuits by Madame de Bullion's uncle, Noël de Sillery. Jeanne stayed at one of two houses built by a prominent colonist, while Maisonneuve and his men settled at nearby St. Michel, where they cut down oaks to build storehouses and boats.

Jeanne soon discovered that the weather was colder, and snowier, than in France. A warm hearth was a necessity to keep everything from freezing, from the food on the table to the inkbottle for writing.

During the long, harsh winter months, Jeanne worked closely with the Natives. She learned to speak their language—no small task considering the many different dialects. They possessed a vast knowledge of local plants and herbs. Jeanne studied their many healing techniques. One of the worst things the Europeans had to endure in Canada was the mosquito. How could they stop the horrible itch? Thankfully, the First Peoples had the answer—a thick coat of bear grease over bare skin.

SLAVERY

As with other colonies, slavery existed in New France. Native slaves, called *Panis*, were usually young, and many died before their eighteenth birthday. Olivier Le Jeune was the first Black slave to be bought in Quebec.

OLIVIER LE JEUNE

A seven-year old boy from Madagascar is believed to have been the first Black slave in Canada. He was sold first to Olivier Le Tardiff and in 1632 to another Quebec resident. He was later educated by the Jesuit priest, Father Le Jeune, and baptized under the name of Olivier Le Jeune. He died a freeman in 1654.

They knew many other remedies, such as boiled sage for coughs or sore throats and white cedar bark to cure scurvy. It was scurvy, a disease brought on by the lack of Vitamin C, usually found in fresh fruits and vegetables, that years earlier had killed twenty-five of Jacques Cartier's men.

The first homes in New France had sloped roofs to prevent snow from piling up. Inside, one large room served as both kitchen and bedroom. Furniture included a master bed for the parents surrounded by the children's little cradles, two or three chairs and the all-important table in the middle. Separate bedrooms were uncommon until the eighteenth century.

Many houses in Montreal resembled small stone fortresses. To protect against raids, slits were built into the walls so the colonists could shoot through them.

Jeanne very quickly took on a position of authority within the colony, helping over the winter to administer provisions to both the soldiers and the colonists, even taking charge of the military stores. The soldiers were building wooden barracks which would later be transported to the new colony at Ville-Marie. The colonists and the soldiers alike respected her and obeyed her as if they were children.

COMMITMENT

Montmagny tried to persuade Maisonneuve to abandon the Ville-Marie expedition and offered the Island of Orleans near Quebec in return. But Maisonneuve, like Jeanne, was committed to Ville-Marie. When the Governor called a meeting to "discuss" the issue, Maisonneuve stated that he was not there to talk, but to carry out orders. "Even if all the trees on the island of Montreal were so many Iroquois," he said, "it is my duty and my honour to go there."

A Birthday Bash

At Jeanne's signal, the cannonballs thundered into the sunrise. A loud crack of fired muskets followed, along with the cheers of Maisonneuve's men. It was January 25, 1642, and Maisonneuve would shortly turn thirty years old. The surprise celebration had been Jeanne's idea. The cannon blasts, however, woke up the Governor of Quebec, Charles Huault de Montmagny. He was very angry. He soon learned of Jeanne Mance's involvement but arrested one of Maisonneuve's men, Jean Gory, and threw him in jail for three days. When Gory was released, Maisonneuve held a feast and added ten crowns to Gory's wages.

"Once we are at Montreal," Maisonneuve boasted to his men, "we shall be our own masters and can fire our cannon when we please."

Despite their differences, Montmagny and Maisonneuve travelled together to the Montreal area that October and chose the future settlement's site.

Ville-Marie, At Last!

Ville-Marie in 1642

Spring arrived, and the Ville-Marie expedition prepared to leave. Madame de La Peltrie was by now so impressed with Jeanne, and eager for an adventure, that she decided to join the expedition. She even took along her furniture, a gesture that inadvertently left the nuns in Quebec, who had been using it, a little upset.

Nevertheless, Jeanne boarded the flat-bottomed boat along with Madame de La Peltrie. The boat, along with two rowboats and a sailboat, set off for the ten-day trip up the St. Lawrence to Ville-Marie.

They arrived on May 17, 1642, a few days earlier than expected. The next day, while Maisonneuve and his men built a wooden altar, Jeanne, Madame de La Peltrie and her servant girl, Charlotte Barré, gathered flowers for its decoration. In a small clearing, Father Vimont, the Jesuit who had accompanied the expedition party, celebrated Mass. As night fell, Jeanne and the others caught fireflies in glass jars and suspended them around the altar.

It was a peaceful beginning for Ville-Marie, but the calm would not last long. The next day, they would start work on a palisade, a fence of sharp wooden stakes, to protect the new settlement.

The First Year

LIVING PURELY

Maisonneuve, Jeanne and the others formed a little group of dedicated Christians who tried to live as purely as they believed the early Christians had lived. The Jesuit priest, Father Vimont, wrote in his *Relations* that "the life they had led in the Fort had been an image of the primitive Church."

Axes sliced through the crisp air as the colonists hacked away at trees. The once tranquil forests of Montreal Island were now filled with the sounds of hard work. Everyone knew that in several months, the St. Lawrence would turn to ice, and snow would blanket the forests. With less than fifty colonists, Ville-Marie quickly became a small outpost about the size of a football field and surrounded by a palisade.

Inside were barracks, a small birchwood chapel, and a few cabins, including one for Jeanne. Her cabin also served as the hospital. Here she tended her first patient, an Algonquin named Patchurini. He recovered within weeks, was baptized and took the new Christian name of Charles.

Cross of Thanks

That December, the St. Lawrence River overflowed, threatening the tiny settlement. The settlers prayed, and by luck, or perhaps a miracle, the river retreated. Ville-Marie had been spared. In early 1643, Maisonneuve and Jeanne led a small pilgrimage up the island's mountain, *la Mont Royal,* or in English, Mount Royal. As a gesture of thanks, Maisonneuve erected a wooden cross, the first to look over what we now call Montreal.

Maisonneuve carries
the cross up Mount Royal

But Ville-Marie would face even more menacing obstacles in the Iroquois. The attacks began in 1643 and continued into the following year. Once, the Iroquois besieged the colonists, killing three and carrying off three more although one managed to escape. Fear of the Iroquois was so great that other Natives living in Ville-Marie decided to leave.

Some of the colonists also gave up, but not Jeanne. Determined as ever, she knew she still had to accomplish her goal—building a true hospital in Ville-Marie.

A Faithful Friend

Maisonneuve jumped to his feet. Pilote, the expedition party's dog, and her puppies were barking loudly at the fort's gate. Maisonneuve

trusted Pilote's keen sense of smell. Her frenzied reaction could only mean one thing: an Iroquois enemy approached.

Within moments, Maisonneuve and thirty of his men had grabbed their weapons and followed Pilote into the snow-covered forest. Many of the soldiers didn't have snowshoes and, after using up all their bullets, they fled, leaving Maisonneuve and Pilote alone against the Iroquois. Fortunately, Maisonneuve still had ammunition left. While Pilote snarled and distracted the Iroquois, he continued to fire his musket as he slowly retreated to the safety of the Fort. Once again, he had survived an Iroquois attack.

The New Hospital

HOSPITAL HOLIDAY

"The sick are well-treated and well-bandaged at Mademoiselle Mance's hospital; she knows how to make their stay a holiday." (Jesuit Relation, 1645)

With more money generously donated by Madame de Bullion, the first Hôtel-Dieu hospital was built two years after Jeanne arrived in Ville-Marie. Today, the spot is at the corner of St. Paul and St. Sulpice streets in Montreal, but at the time, Hôtel-Dieu was only a short walk from the Fort. It had a kitchen, two sick rooms, a small room for Jeanne and another for a helper, all in an area the size of a backyard swimming pool. Like the Fort, the little hospital was surrounded by a watery ditch and a cedar palisade for protection.

That summer, the Society of Our Lady of Montreal sent Jeanne a shipload of supplies. Along with medicines, linens, surgical instruments, furniture and copper pots, were two oxen, three cows and twenty sheep.

The first Hôtel-Dieu hospital at the site of the present-day Hôtel-Dieu

Daily Cares

SAGAMITÉ

Native peoples often made a staple meal called sagamité. Corn was dried, pounded and boiled into a porridge to which beans, squash and assorted game meat or fish were added.

Jeanne rose before dawn, as usual. After prayers, she checked on her still-sleeping patients. On one rope bed, a little Algonquin girl coughed, her worried mother at her side. Jeanne took a wooden bowl from the wall and stepped outside. The rain barrel was full; there was enough water for laundry and a sagamité, flavoured with the European salt and spices that intrigued the First Peoples.

Jeanne scooped some water for the sick child into the bowl and sighed. If only Madame de La Peltrie hadn't been recalled to Quebec. The women of the Fort, such as the Native child's grateful mother, helped out with the cooking and daily chores, but Jeanne knew the work would have been easier if her close friend had stayed.

Eels and Pemmican

Meals consisted of whatever was available such as squash, pumpkins and corn during the harvest. Eels and freshly-caught rabbits were plentiful. Other meats included moose, venison, salted or smoked pork and wildfowl in a *tourtière* (or pie) for a treat. As Roman Catholics, the colonists observed days of fasting. On Fridays and during Lent, they were not allowed to eat any meat except fish and seafood. The Church did permit beaver or otter though because, they reasoned, those animals spent much of their lives in water.

Once Jeanne and Maisonneuve arranged a feast in front of Hôtel-Dieu for the First Nations, including many reluctant Iroquois. The Natives filled half a dozen boilers with water, corn, prunes and raisins, as well as various meats including bear, even a couple of fat cats and a dog. To honour Jeanne Mance and the others, the chiefs insisted the Europeans have the first portions. Jeanne carefully ate the unusual "sagamité" so as not to offend anyone.

THE FRENCHMAN'S MOOSE

On June 25, 1647, a horse was brought over from France to Quebec as a gift for Governor Montmagny. The First Peoples had never seen such an animal before and called it the "Frenchman's Moose".

Trying Times

TORTURE

The Iroquois captured Father Jean de Brébeuf and another Jesuit, Jérôme Lalemant, in 1649. The priests were tied to poles and tortured for hours. Although they killed Brébeuf, the Iroquois respected his courage and ritually consumed his heart to acquire some of his bravery. In 1930, Brébeuf and Lalemant were canonized as saints by the Catholic Church.

THE HURON CAROL

As a gift to the First Peoples, Brébeuf wrote Canada's first Christmas carol, the Huron Carol.

Sample of the text:

T'was in the moon of winter time, when all the birds had fled,
That mighty Gitchi-Manitou sent angel choirs instead,
Before their light the stars grew dim, and wondering hunters heard the hymn:
Jesus your King is born, Jesus is born, in excelcis gloria.

In 1649, word arrived from France that Father Rapine had died, and the Society of Our Lady was in ruins. Many were losing faith in Ville-Marie. A brief truce with the Iroquois four years earlier had long since failed. Fighting had reached new heights.

That fall, Jeanne made a crucial trip back to France.

Once again, she captured the nobility's interest and even met Queen Anne of Austria, the mother of the future King Louis XIV of France. Jeanne's efforts to gather support succeeded, but when she returned to New France the following spring, she received terrible news: tribal raids and massacres had virtually wiped out the Wendat peoples.

The martyr Father Jean de Brébeuf

32

Chiquot

Despite the dangers, Jeanne had not hesitated to return to Ville-Marie. With only fifty colonists in the settlement, Jeanne knew she would often be alone at Hôtel-Dieu. Daily life in Ville-Marie was always a risk and everyone, whether asleep in a cabin or outside planting crops, lived under the threat of attack.

During one raid in the spring of 1651, a colonist named Jean Boudart was killed and his wife, Catherine, kidnapped. Others heard her screams and ran out to help. With muskets they had obtained from the Dutch, the Iroquois fought back. Fortunately, Jeanne had left Hôtel-Dieu unlocked, and the colonists quickly took refuge in the hospital. Behind the firmly barred doors, they exchanged fire through the windows. A ball shot from one Native musket passed through a colonist's hat, narrowly missing his head. Finally, the Iroquois, who really had no idea how many were in the hospital, left.

One colonist, named Chiquot, had been half-scalped and left for dead in the fields. He managed to survive and crawl back to the hospital. Jeanne immediately prepared a needle to stitch his gaping wound. Thanks to her remarkable skills, Chiquot recovered and lived fourteen more years.

33

22,000 Livres

The raids continued daily, and Maisonneuve ordered all the colonists in Ville-Marie to abandon their homes. Everyone was forced to stay in the Fort. At least a hundred soldiers were needed to protect the settlement, but Ville-Marie had only seventeen trained men. Maisonneuve was adamant: new recruits from France were vital. But who would pay for them? The little settlement seemed doomed.

"Every person was discouraged," wrote Jeanne. "I felt what a loss it would be to religion and what a disgrace for the State if it had to lose the colony after all we had done; I therefore urged Maisonneuve to go to France for help."

A sketch made by the explorer Champlain, depicting an Iroquois defeat

If the colony could not survive, Jeanne reasoned, neither could the hospital. She made a bold decision and gave Maisonneuve the money, 22,000 *livres* reserved for the hospital ($150,000 dollars in today's money but worth much more then). The money, she explained, was to be used to hire recruits. Yet Jeanne did not stop there. She felt that, just this once, she might have to break her oath. The "unknown benefactress" of Ville-Marie, she confided to Maisonneuve, was the wealthy Parisian widow, Madame de Bullion.

Keeping a Secret

When Maisonneuve arrived in France, he accompanied his sister, a nun, to Madame de Bullion's home. The visit was regarding another matter, but Maisonneuve knew that once he said the words, "New France", Madame de Bullion would be intrigued.

Without letting on that he knew her secret, Maisonneuve spoke of his work in New France. He told Madame de Bullion how a brave woman named Jeanne Mance, funded by a secret benefactress, had sent him to Paris with 22,000 *livres* to hire recruits. The money, he explained, was to have been used for a hospital, but Mademoiselle Mance had said that if her "unknown benefactress" were aware of Ville-Marie's plight, she would give her consent and perhaps more funds. In exchange for this money, Maisonneuve added, he had personally provided Jeanne with one hundred acres of land to build the hospital.

Madame de Bullion was now informed— and it appeared that Jeanne had kept her word. While the wealthy widow never did reveal to Maisonneuve that she was the "unknown benefactress", she made certain that another donation of 20,000 *livres* arrived, once again anonymously, for Hôtel-Dieu.

Left to Burn

DIVINE INTERVENTION

In the spring of 1653, Jeanne stopped at Trois-Rivières on her way to Quebec. Perhaps it was simply luck, or, as Jeanne believed, divine intervention, but she left only two days before six hundred Iroquois warriors attacked Trois-Rivières and killed many colonists.

Jeanne clutched her cape tighter, trying to stay warm in the brisk late September air. Maisonneuve and his recruits had still not arrived, and she wondered what had happened. Finally, his ship came into sight but stopped short of the port. Passengers disembarked into rowboats and brought the sorry news: illnesses on board had claimed many lives, the ship was riddled with disease and had struck a reef.

Maisonneuve was safe, but all agreed that the entire ship had to be torched.

Despite the dismal start, the one hundred and five recruits immediately set out to keep Iroquois raiders under control. For Ville-Marie, the newly-arrived support meant that abandoned houses could be reopened and fields prepared for crops. Maisonneuve now knew that the settlement was safe. Among the items he brought back from France were a chalice and tapestry for the first stone chapel in Montreal, Notre-Dame-de-Bon-Secours.

Marguerite Bourgeoys

CANADA'S SAINT

Marguerite established the Congregation of Notre-Dame. She became Canada's first woman saint.

Born in 1620, Marguerite, like Jeanne, first came to Canada in her early thirties. Maisonneuve's sister had proposed to the Society of Our Lady that a school be set up in Ville-Marie where colonist and Native children could be educated for free. Marguerite was chosen to organize the project.

In France, Maisonneuve arranged for her to join him on the return voyage. When they met, Marguerite instantly recognized him, although they had never met. "I have had visions," she said. "You were in them, and my dreams have told me to go to New France."

For a school, Marguerite was given an old stone stable not far from Jeanne's Hôtel-Dieu. After cleaning it up, Marguerite hired men to install a chimney and repair the roof. A sleeping area was made out of the former dovecote (a shelter for doves and pigeons) under the roof, while the lower rooms were used for the school and living quarters. On April 30, 1658, three girls and five boys attended the first class in Ville-Marie. The once deserted building soon became a busy home, where new settlers were welcomed, children learned, and various meetings were held.

Truce

SETTLING IN

Fourteen marriages were registered in 1655, the same year Isabelle and Marie Moyen came to Jeanne. Like most girls in New France, the sisters eventually married and had children. At the age of sixteen, Isabelle wed a man twenty-three years her senior. Years later, Jeanne became godmother to Marie Moyen's baby.

WAMPUM BELT

The First Peoples used the wampum belt as a promise symbol. Made from the inner part of shells, each bead colour and row had a special meaning. The Treaty Belt had two rows of purple beads, one for each party, separated by three rows of white beads representing peace, a good mind and empowerment.

Frequent Iroquois raids continued to threaten the early existence of Ville-Marie, but there were attempts at peace, usually with prisoner exchanges.

During one brief truce, four new orphans were put under Jeanne's care. Among them were two young girls, Isabelle and Marie Moyen. They had seen their parents killed in a raid before being taken themselves. Women and children prisoners were often "adopted" by Natives after battles. Not only did it comfort already bereaved members of the tribe, it helped keep their population from declining, especially after losing many to epidemics.

Although she never had children of her own, Jeanne quickly earned a reputation as the "mother of the colony". Not only was she named as godmother to babies more than forty times during her life, but she willingly took in anyone, adult or child, who needed help.

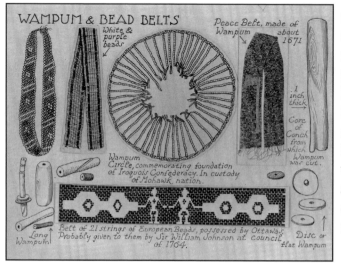

A Bad Fall

ETIENNE BOUCHARD

Etienne Bouchard came to New France with Maisonneuve in 1653. By 1665, he was Montreal's chief physician and was paid by the citizens a fee of one hundred *livres* a year for his medical services.

On January 28, 1657, despite freezing conditions, Jeanne set out to visit a sick colonist. Along the way, she slipped on a patch of ice, breaking her right arm and dislocating her wrist. Neighbours rushed her to Hôtel-Dieu, but when Ville-Marie's surgeon, Étienne Bouchard arrived, Jeanne lay unconscious from the pain.

Word spread quickly about Jeanne's accident. The Governor General in Quebec even sent his own personal surgeon to help her. Jeanne's fractures eventually healed, but her wrist had not set properly. The injury left her arm virtually useless. Jeanne later wrote: "From the moment of my fracture, I could not use my arm. I had to be dressed and served like a child."

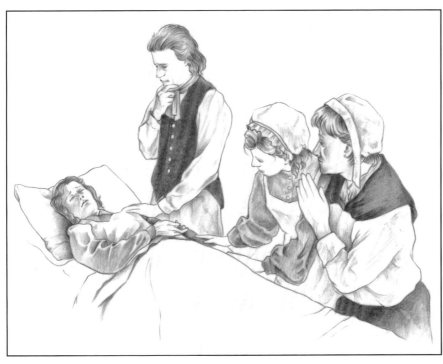

My Home is Your Home

THE SULPICIANS

In 1641, a French priest named Jean-Jacques Olier founded the Seminary of St. Sulpice outside Paris. His goal was to reform the clergy, and eventually the Church in France, by establishing a new order, the Sulpicians—priests dedicated to educating fellow priests through a simple lifestyle based on selfless devotion to God.

GABRIEL SOUART

One of the new arrivals, Gabriel Souart, was a French tobacco businessman before he became a Sulpician priest. He was Ville-Marie's first priest, and, with permission from the Pope, eventually practised medicine in the colony.

Back in France, the Sulpician founder, Father Olier, had become gravely ill. Before he died, Olier appointed a priest, Father Gabriel de Queylus, to take three other Sulpicians and accompany Maisonneuve on one of his voyages back to Ville-Marie. They reached New France in August, 1657. Eighteen passengers had perished during the crossing, victims of a typhus outbreak on board.

Jeanne warmly welcomed the tired priests. She also offered them her home until a Seminary (a school that trains students to be priests) was built years later.

Jean-Jacques Olier

Power Struggles

The Hôtel-Dieu hospital in Ville-Marie now needed more nurses. In particular, they wanted the *Hospitalières* of St. Joseph

stationed at La Flèche, France, and as soon as possible. Jeanne and Marguerite were to travel back to France for them, but just as they prepared to leave, Father de Queylus sent two Augustinian nuns from the Hôtel-Dieu in Quebec to Ville-Marie. Their stay was supposed to be temporary but de Queylus, like many others, felt the Augustinian nuns should eventually control Jeanne's Hôtel-Dieu.

Jeanne didn't know it, but de Queylus had also written a letter to La Dauversière, the founder of the *Hospitalières de St-Joseph* in La Flèche, suggesting this arrangement. He even said that Jeanne approved.

Nothing could have been further from the truth.

THE HOSPITALIÈRES OF ST. JOSEPH

Founded in 1636 at La Flèche, France, the Congregation of the Daughters *Hospitalières* of Saint Joseph (the *Hospitalières*) were nuns dedicated to serving the sick, poor and those "without hearth or home". By doing so, they helped establish Hôtel-Dieu hospitals throughout France, Canada and the United States. Now known as the Religious *Hospitalières* of St. Joseph, or RHSJ, they still continue their compassionate work to this day in various places around the world.

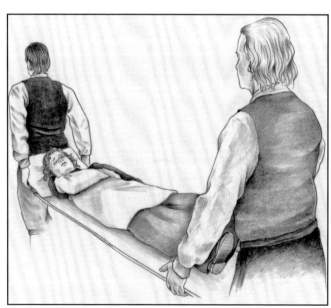

Back to France

Jeanne and Marguerite Bourgeoys returned to France the following year. With her arm constantly in a sling, Jeanne was grateful for Marguerite's company. To have someone help her with the simplest tasks like dressing and washing must have made the long journey that much more bearable.

In France, La Dauversière had already received de Queylus's letter. Jeanne quickly explained the situation and Ville-Marie's urgent need for the *Hospitalières* from La Flèche. Plans were set in motion.

Three nuns, Judie Moreau de Brésoles, Catherine Macé and Marie Maillet were chosen for Hôtel-Dieu. Once there, they would serve the sick, both colonists and First Peoples, free of charge, while Jeanne would remain the hospital's administrator for as long as she lived.

Jeanne's efforts were getting results, but physically, she was suffering. Sometimes, the pain of her arm injury was so unbearable that she had to be carried on a stretcher. She consulted the best doctors in Paris, but they all came to the same conclusion—nothing could be done.

A Miracle?

An early 20th century illustration of Jeanne Mance

DE CASSON

Dollier de Casson, a Sulpician priest and historian, became the Seigneur of Montreal in 1670. He personally saw Jeanne's statement. "If the handwriting has some faults," he wrote, "the blame is to be placed on the extreme joy with which she was moved and not on the weakness of the arm and of the hand."

In Paris, Jeanne arranged to visit the Seminary of St. Sulpice. Marguerite was away seeking more recruits, so Jeanne went alone. She walked through the courtyard, past the tomb of Father Olier, and into the empty chapel, where the Superior of the Seminary awaited her. Even though all the others were at a religious ceremony, he said Mass, gave Jeanne Holy Communion, then briefly left. He returned with a metal box containing the preserved heart of Father Olier.

Jeanne cradled the precious relic in her good arm while the Superior left her alone to pray. In a letter she later wrote to Marguerite, Jeanne described a moment of intense joy, like nothing she had ever felt before, and how her once useless arm became functional and free of pain.

Jeanne immediately fetched the Superior and told him of her miracle. At his request, she wrote the following translated:

Jesus, Marie, Joseph, the 2nd of February, 1659, in the chapel of the Seminary, I wrote these words after Holy Mass, with my right hand of which for two years I had not any use.

Word spread quickly. Doctors attested to Jeanne's miraculous cure. Children cut off pieces of her dress for relics. Jeanne welcomed the renewed interest in her cause, but couldn't wait to get back to Ville-Marie.

From La Flèche to La Rochelle

With more funds from Madame de Bullion, Jeanne travelled to La Flèche, France. There she met with the three nuns from the Congregation of the Daughters *Hospitalières* of Saint Joseph, the order originally founded by La Dauversière and Marie de La Ferre. Jeanne planned to accompany the nuns back to Ville-Marie, where they would work as nurses.

Even with the Church's permission, many in France did not want their sisters and daughters to leave their homeland. Some thought that La Dauversière had brain-washed the young women. As the *Hospitalières* prepared to depart, a mob gathered. Forced to draw their swords, their escorts cleared the way for them to pass through.

When they arrived at the port of La Rochelle, the captain of the *St-André* refused to set sail. Rumours had spread that the women couldn't pay their passage. Fortunately, one of the *Hospitalières* had sewn money into the bodice of her dress. Jeanne convinced a local merchant to give the Captain a promissory note for the remainder and, finally, the ship left port.

Joining the *Hospitalières* were sixty-two men, forty-seven women and eight children willing to settle in Ville-Marie. Jeanne had lent many of them money for the passage. Preserved documents show that all paid her back in full.

The *Hospitalières* are sent on their way in the midst of the mob

ANOTHER FALL

On the trip to La Flèche, Jeanne rode on horseback. At one point, the horse reared and Jeanne fell. She landed directly on her right arm but was unhurt. Jeanne believed this was more proof that her cure was no less than a miracle.

A Difficult Voyage on the *St-André*

POWER STRUGGLES

Quebec did not officially become a Church diocese until 1674, but when Bishop François de Laval arrived in 1659, he asserted his authority right away. A power struggle between Laval and the current Governor of New France, Pierre de Voyer d'Argenson, soon began. The Jesuit *Relations* of 1660 described one tense religious procession which both Laval and d'Argenson said they would not attend unless they were greeted first. It was finally agreed that "the children's hands should be kept occupied so that neither one nor the other would be greeted." Some children, however, were prompted by their parents to greet the Governor first, and despite the Jesuits' pleas, were whipped for disobeying.

Raging Atlantic storms kept the one hundred and fifty passengers below deck for days on end. Unable to sleep, constantly seasick, and tossed out of their bunks, they wondered if each day at sea would be their last.

They arrived in New France seventy-one days later. Eleven people had died on the voyage. Seriously ill herself, Jeanne remained in Quebec but implored the three *Hospitalières* to ask Bishop Laval for permission to continue on to Montreal. Weeks passed, with Laval constantly urging the *Hospitalières* to stay and join the Augustinian Sisters in Quebec. Undaunted, the *Hospitalières* refused to waver from the oath they had taken at La Flèche to travel on to Ville-Marie.

Bishop François
Montmorency de Laval

45

The *Hospitalières* Arrive

THE GOOD MOTHERS

Marie de l'Incarnation was one of the few in Quebec who supported the *Hospitalières*. On Sept.17, 1660, she wrote: "The good Mothers *Hospitalières* who came last year to settle in Montreal were nearly going back to France as their funds were seized and considered lost. But Monseigneur our Prelate kept them at the persistent request of the inhabitants of Montreal; for they are persons of great virtue and edification."

A stained glass window in Notre-Dame Cathedral in Montreal depicting Jeanne Mance

After a month in Quebec, Laval finally consented; the *Hospitalières* were free to journey to Ville-Marie.

The settlement's two hundred inhabitants greeted them warmly, but because of a busy harvest, they hadn't had time to build their lodgings. Jeanne's arrival a little later quickly changed that and, at her insistence, additions to Hôtel-Dieu were soon constructed.

The new buildings became the heart of Ville-Marie. Attached to a chapel, the two-storey stone and wood building was separated into two wards on the ground floor, six beds for the men and two for the women. A fireplace at each end served for both cooking and warmth, while Sister Brésoles used one corner for a small apothecary.

The Sisters slept in a small room divided into tiny "cells" on the top floor. Each morning, they ducked to avoid the damp linens hung throughout their quarters to dry and quietly descended the twenty-two steps to the patients' floor. As one Sister mentioned, there was always "very little linen and many wounded".

Early that November, word came from France that La Dauversière had died. Much of Hôtel-Dieu's money, given to Jeanne by Madame de Bullion, had gone straight to paying off his large debt. Unable to support them, the Société de Notre-Dame urged the *Hospitalières* to return to France. But with Jeanne's encouragement, they firmly resolved to stay.

Years of Poverty

CANADA'S FIRST WRITER

Marie Morin was born in Quebec less than ten years after Jeanne had first arrived in Montreal. While training to become a nun, Marie lived and worked with Jeanne for eleven years.

The *Annals of Hôtel-Dieu* were originally written for Sister Morin's religious Sisters. It wasn't until almost two hundred years after her death that the *Annals* were printed as a book. Marie Morin was the first Canadian-born *Hospitalière* but, in many ways, she can also be considered Canada's first writer.

FANCY CLOTHES

Maisonneuve preferred a simple grey country cape to fancy clothes. On one voyage from France, he claimed to have "mislaid his official apparel of lace and fine linen" and was "very pleased to be well-rid of all those vain ornaments."

Jeanne and the *Hospitalières* never had much money. They lived off charitable donations, such as the yearly five hundred *livres* from the priests of St. Sulpice in Paris. They scraped by on whatever food was available. Hostilities with the Iroquois made venturing out into the woods to hunt, or even pick berries, very dangerous. In her journal, *Annals of Hôtel-Dieu*, Sister Marie Morin wrote, "I assure you, my sisters, that for ten years I have had no fruit, except for wild plums once or twice a year."

Winter was especially difficult. Drifting snow blew through the cracks of the cabin walls. The Sisters spent each morning shovelling out and thawing food that had frozen overnight. With no money, they patched their clothes with whatever rags were left.

"Your clothes have so many repairs," Maisonneuve once joked with the Sisters, "that I cannot tell what the original dress looked like." That prompted Jeanne to point out the patches she could identify from her old dresses. The former governor's wife, Madame d'Ailleboust, joined in and announced that she too could spot those that once belonged to her. Their hearty laughter went a long way towards easing their daily struggles and a poverty-stricken situation that was to last almost three decades.

In 1660, Adam Dollard des Ormeaux and seventeen soldiers left Montreal to fight the Iroquois. Ambushed near Long Sault, they hid in an old cabin for a full week before the Iroquois finally defeated and killed them.

Ville-Marie in 1650

FIRST HOUSES

Louis d'Ailleboust was the Governor of Quebec who succeeded Montmagny and the first colonist to sow French grain in Canada. His wife, Barbe, was a devout woman who had learned the Algonquin language. When Louis died in 1660, she went to live with the *Hospitalières* in Ville-Marie. As a wealthy widow, she helped build Ville-Marie's first houses on Saint-Joseph Street.

Constant Fear

Jeanne made certain that the *Hospitalières* treated everyone—colonists, First Peoples, even Iroquois wounded during their raids on the settlement. During these attacks, Sisters Morin and Brésoles would run up to the belfry. When the warning bell rang, Sister Maillet sometimes fainted, and Sister Macé hid near the Chapel, paralysed with fear.

"From our high station, we could sometimes see the combat, which terrified us extremely, so that we came down again as soon as we could, trembling with fright, and thinking that our last hour was come," wrote Sister Marie Morin.

One colonist found a creative way to protect himself during the raids. Mathurin Jouaneaux was an experienced axe-man who had signed a contract to work for five years clearing land. Since the land he was given to cultivate wasn't near the fort, he found a hollowed tree trunk, dug a small cave under it and covered the entrance with brush. As soon as the belfry sounded, he quickly hopped into his secret shelter.

Later, while building a barn, Jouaneaux slipped from the roof and injured himself. Nursed back to health by the *Hospitalières* of Hôtel-Dieu, Jouaneaux was so grateful that he gave them all of his land and buildings and spent the rest of his life working at the Hôtel-Dieu.

Firewater

This drawing by a Jesuit missionary in 1657 shows a Wendat family praying after their conversion to Christianity.

VILE FUR TRADERS

"Had it not been for the vileness of the Companies' agents, and the treachery of the paid servants of the traders, perhaps Fathers Lalement and de Brébeuf would never have been martyred by the irritated Iroquois."

-Marie de l'Incarnation

EXCOMMUNICATION

Excommunication is a punishment whereby a person is banned from the Roman Catholic Church for their sins.

Most of the merchant companies and fur trade workers disapproved of the faith-driven missionaries like the Jesuits, Marguerite Bourgeoys and Jeanne Mance. They worried that educated Natives would demand more in return for the furs they trapped, or worse yet, stop trapping altogether. The liquor the French gave them kept the Natives dependent, and the traders made sure they were given lots of "firewater".

Fighting between the French, their Native allies and the Iroquois intensified and ultimately, the Governor of Quebec, Pierre Dubois d'Avaugour, (called "Ontonio" or "big mountain" by the Natives, a name they gave to important French governors), imposed severe penalties on those who trafficked in liquor. Punishment included whipping, imprisonment and even death. Unfortunately, most colonists were guilty of the crime. When one priest pleaded on behalf of an imprisoned woman, d'Avaugour was furious. He decreed that if liquor trafficking wasn't a crime for her, then it wasn't for anyone in the colony.

Frustrated, Bishop Laval tried to impose excommunication on liquor smugglers. Nevertheless, firewater flowed freely. It seemed that nothing could stop it.

Earthquake!

METEOR

"A great globe of flame which threw out sparks on all sides".

That was the description of what was seen one night in 1663. It was probably a meteor, but during the seventeenth century, unusual displays in the heavens were thought to be signs of bad things to come.

Two days before the start of Lent, in the pre-dawn hours of February 5, 1663, a tremendous roar echoed through New France. Walls shook violently. Uprooted trees crashed to the ground. Jolted awake, the colonists rushed outside. Unable to stand on the trembling earth, they tumbled into the snow.

Sisters de Brésoles, Macé and Maillet were already in the chapel for morning prayers but froze with fear when the earthquake began. Father Souart, the priest, yelled for them to get out, in case the roof caved in. Wearing only her nightclothes, Madame d'Ailleboust, widow of the late governor D'Ailleboust, ran outside, only to see the ground split open near her bare feet.

Aftershocks shook New France for seven more months. Mudslides into the St. Lawrence River left the water temporarily undrinkable. Miraculously, no one had perished. It was, the colonists thought, as if God had given them one last chance to renounce their sins. As Lent progressed, more people fasted, made confession and attended church. Both Laval and D'Avaugour took advantage of the situation and preached the evils of the liquor trade. This time, the colonists listened.

Final Voyage

GOVERNMENT

New France was similar to a French province. The King's representative and commander of the army was the Governor, but it was the Intendant who controlled civilian affairs and made sure the King's wishes were implemented. Soldier recruits protected the colony from Iroquois raids, and trade was managed by the large *Compagnie des Indes occidentales* (West Indies Company).

MONEY

Coins were not made in New France; they came from the mother country. In 1685, card money was introduced because of the lack of coins and other currency. They were used like an IOU or post-dated cheque is today.

Jeanne wasn't in New France during the earthquake. She had left for France a few months earlier. Now fifty-four years old, Jeanne prepared to act as Maisonneuve's representative and formally hand over control of Ville-Marie to the Order of St. Sulpice. King Louis XIV officially declared New France a crown colony in 1663. No longer needed, the Society of Montreal dissolved. Ville-Marie was secure, but missionary work was no longer a priority.

Back in France, those still dedicated to the original plan for Ville-Marie were encouraged to send over young girls interested in becoming nuns. More than twenty arrived. Most had intended to join the *Hospitalières* but ended up married to colonists instead.

An assortment of original 1685 playing card money

52

FILLES DU ROI

The first population census of Canada was taken in 1660. New France had 3,418 people—one woman for every six men.

Each *fille du roi* was given a small money-box, a taffeta kerchief, shoe ribbons, sewing needles, thread and scissors, a comb, stockings, gloves, knives, pins, a bonnet and two silver coins. Once married, she received a dowry or gift from the King, usually fifty *livres*, or if she were well-born, twice that amount.

A painting by an early 20th century Canadian artist showing the *filles du roi* arriving in Quebec in 1667, in order to be married to French Canadian farmers. They are being welcomed by Talon and Laval. It is, however, unlikely that the poor young women arriving in Quebec in the mid-1600s looked as fashionable or as self-confident as these.

The King's Daughters

Jeanne was disappointed, but not surprised, that the *Hospitalières* of St. Joseph had few recruits. Surviving in the new colony was difficult enough; dedicating one's life to serving the sick was even more demanding. Most of the young women who came to New France between 1634 and 1662 were under twenty-five years old, poor and either servants or orphans. Some, usually those from Paris, married in Quebec, then went back to France with their husbands.

In 1662, the minister in charge of the colonies, Jean Colbert, sought strong young girls to be sent to New France for marriage. Over the next ten years, more than eight hundred young women arrived. They were called the *filles du roi*—the King's Daughters.

Once in New France, the girls were put under a nun's care before being officially presented to eligible colonists. After a few weeks, many were formally engaged. A *fille du roi* was free to marry whomever she wished, and annulment was possible if she soon discovered that she had made a mistake.

One girl, who arrived in 1661, married in October, received an annulment in January, quickly got engaged to another man, then changed her mind and married someone else that summer. She and her husband eventually had eleven children.

The Last Years

The last ten years of Jeanne's life were perhaps her most difficult. In 1665, Maisonneuve was removed as Governor of Montreal and sent back to France. Jeanne and the *Hospitalières* missed him dearly, especially his ability to make them laugh and forget their troubles.

A FOUNDATION STONE

On June 30, 1672, a thousand people, almost the entire population of Montreal, gathered for a special celebration. After Mass, they proceeded to the site of the new Notre-Dame Parish Church. Dollier de Casson blessed five foundation stones, each inscribed with an important name in Montreal's history: that of the Governor General, the Governor of Montreal, the Intendant, the Superior of the Seminary, and finally, that of Jeanne Mance.

Another problem concerned land disputes between the Sulpicians and Bishop Laval. Jeanne was caught up in the legalities, and the case went all the way to the King's Privy Council. The matter was eventually resolved, but Jeanne was soon resigned to the fact that Montreal wasn't exactly the "City of God" that she and Maisonneuve had hoped for.

It saddened Jeanne that the colony was no longer referred to as Ville-Marie. As the population increased, so did the troubles. Crime and disease thrived in the now crowded, muddy streets.

A Life Well-Lived

June 3, 1669—A portion of Jeanne's will from the Montreal Archives

As her health rapidly declined, Jeanne now spent most of her time bed-ridden, left to pray or reminisce about her life and friends, many of whom had already passed away. Knowing that she was losing her strength, she wrote her will in 1669 and, a few years later, added a clause agreeing to leave her heart to her beloved Ville-Marie.

Soon, the woman who had devoted her life to caring for others, could not even care for herself. On the morning of Sunday, June 18, 1673, Jeanne passed away. She was buried under the hospital chapel, but her heart was placed in a metal container and put under the sanctuary in the chapel until it could be transferred to the new church. It was a Catholic tradition to preserve the heart, a symbol of love for Christ, especially of devout persons such as Jeanne.

Unfortunately, a fire destroyed the chapel, and heart, in 1695. Below ground, her coffin remained untouched, and today rests under the present Hôtel-Dieu on Pine Avenue in Montreal.

Angel of the Colony

A 1973 stamp
honouring Jeanne Mance

TRADITION OF CARING

Today, Hôtel-Dieu in Montreal is often called "the Motherhouse" to the other sixty institutions founded by the *Religieuses Hospitalières de Saint-Joseph* (RHSJ) throughout the world.

"She possessed a charming grace, a fine and noble bearing, an attractive personality, keen wit, and above all, was gifted with natural eloquence."

-Sister Marie Morin

Jeanne Mance would be surprised to hear the many titles given to her today. Among others, she is known as the co-founder of Montreal, first woman missionary in Canada, and first lay nurse in Canada, in fact, in all of North America. Her name has graced awards, parks, streets, schools, residences, and, in Ottawa, the first government building to be named after a woman. She is a model for nurses across the country and a true Canadian hero.

Of all her honours, perhaps Jeanne would feel the most comfortable being remembered as the "Angel of the Colony". Her strength came from her faith in that fledgling settlement called Ville-Marie. Throughout her life, Jeanne's only desire was to serve others, especially the colony she believed in, to the best of her ability. She succeeded, and Canada will forever be grateful to the young girl who, long ago, vowed to care.

The corner of Rue Jeanne-Mance and
Rue Maisonneuve in Montreal

A statue of
Jeanne Mance
in Montreal

Jeanne's life and times

1606	November 12, the infant Jeanne Mance is baptized in Langres, France.
1613	Jeanne becomes a student at the Ursuline School in Langres.
1640	After speaking with her cousin, Nicolas Dolebeau, Jeanne travels to Paris for advice about missionary work in New France.
1641	Madame de Bullion asks Jeanne Mance to found a hospital in Canada. Jeanne meets Jérôme de Royer de La Dauversière and joins the "Montreal Expedition" led by Paul de Chomedey de Maisonneuve. The expedition arrives in New France (Quebec) that August.
1642	Ville-Marie founded. Jeanne lives and works out of a small dispensary within the Fort.
1643	Jeanne treats the Algonquin chief, Patchurini.
1644	200 Iroquois attack the Fort.
1645	A new Hôtel-Dieu hospital is built near the Fort.
1648	In the *Société de Notre Dame de Montréal* contract, Jeanne is made administrator of the hospital.
1649	Jeanne returns to France.
1650	60,000 *livres* (pounds) and 200 *arpents* (acres) acquired for Ville-Marie.
1651	Chiquot is treated by Jeanne. He lives fourteen years longer. The Iroquois raids increase and threaten the survival of Ville-Marie. Jeanne gives the 22,000 *livres* saved for the future Hôtel-Dieu to Maisonneuve so he can acquire 100 new recruits for Ville-Marie.
1653	Maisonneuve arrives with the recruits and Marguerite Bourgeoys.
1657	Jeanne falls on ice and injures her right arm. Arrival of Abbé de Queylus and three other Sulpician priests
1658	Jeanne's second voyage to France

1659	"Miraculous" cure of Jeanne's arm With three *Hospitalières* of Saint Joseph from La Flèche, Jeanne returns to New France.
1660	Jeanne learns of the death of La Dauversière.
1661-62	The *Hospitalières* are finally given Church approval.
1662	Jeanne's last voyage to France.
1663	Louis XIV declares Ville-Marie, now called Montreal, a royal colony. In Paris, Jeanne is witness as it is now placed under the care of the Order of Saint-Sulpice.
1665	Paul de Chomedey de Maisonneuve returns to France.
1669	Jeanne writes her will.
1672	Jeanne helps lay one of five foundation stones for Notre-Dame church.
1673	Jeanne dies on June 18, and her heart is preserved in the Hôtel-Dieu chapel.

About the Author

Joanna Emery was born in England, but moved to Ottawa at a young age. From early childhood, Joanna was instilled with a deep sense of curiosity, a passion for history, and a love of writing.

In 1989, Joanna graduated with a Bachelor of Humanities from McMaster University with a major in history. Her first picture book, *Melville Smellville* (Small World Publishing, Nova Scotia), was released in 2001. Joanna's second book, *Brothers of the Falls* (Silver Moon Press), a middle-grade historical novel set in 1847 Niagara Falls, was published in 2004. She has also authored three early readers due out in 2006, *Antonio's Music*, a biography of composer Antonio Vivaldi (Scholastic), and *Louis Cyr*, a biography of Canada's nineteenth-century strong man (Scholastic).

She has received two awards for her work. She is the winner of Best Non-Fiction Article by the Hamilton & Region Literary Awards, and the Frances E. Russell Award for outstanding research for a work of Canadian children's literature. She lives in southwestern Ontario with her husband and their three children.

Acknowledgements

The author would like to thank the following for their assistance in the research of this book: In Montreal, Sister Thérèse Payer (RHSJ), Sister Nicole Bussières (RHSJ), the Centre Jeanne-Mance, Musée des *Hospitalières* de l'Hôtel-Dieu de Montrèal, and in Kingston, Sister Loretta Gaffney (RHSJ), the St. Joseph Regional House, and Rodney Carter, Archivist, St. Joseph Region Archives.

Some Terms Explained

Apothecary: a pharmacy, from the Greek for "to put away"; usually a cabinet or box with small storage drawers to contain medicines, tonics and herbs

Armoire: large wardrobe with doors; originally from cupboards used to store "armour"

Arpent: a unit to measure length, similar to modern terms such as an acre or hectare

Bishop: In 17th century New France, he was the Pope's representative as head of the Catholic Church in New France, appointed by the King

Cloistered: a term used to describe a religious order (usually nuns) that took solemn vows to remain in a convent and not go outside without permisssion. The RHSJ were cloistered until 1925

Compagnie des Cent-Associés: Company of One Hundred Associates, the company that owned New France from 1627 to 1663 and had a monopoly over its fur trade. It was replaced in 1663 by the Compagnie des Indes Occidentales.

Coureur des bois: literally, "runner of the woods", an unlicensed fur trader who worked closely with the Natives

Governor General: King's representative and highest dignitary in New France, controlled the military

Hospitalières: the French term for nuns dedicated to serving the sick. In New France, Augustinian nuns worked at the Hôtel-Dieu hospital in Quebec while in Ville-Marie (Montreal) it was the Congregation of the Daughters Hospitalières of Saint Joseph, known today as the Religious Hospitalières of Saint Joseph (RHSJ).

Île d'Orléans: island near Quebec City in the St. Lawrence River. In 1650, it was called Île Sainte-Marie when populated by the Wendat (Huron), before the tribe was massacred by the Iroquois in 1656.

Intendant: appointed by the King, he administered the justice, internal affairs and finances of New France

Jesuits: Society of Jesus. The missionaries of a religious order in New France

Layperson: a spiritually devout person who is not a member of a religious order

La Société de Notre-Dame de Montréal: the Society of Our Lady of Montreal

Livres: basis of the French monetary system: one livre was worth 20 "sols"; one sol was worth 12 "deniers"

Pemmican: nourishing Native food of dried meat and berries

Récollet: the first missionaries on the St. Lawrence, they arrived in 1615 with Champlain

Sagamité: a nourishing soup made from Indian corn flour, fish and dried peas

Seigneurial System: land in New France was divided into sections called seigneuries; these were settled and farmed by tenants (or habitants) who, in turn, paid dues (usually a portion of their harvest) to the legal landowners or seigneurs.

Sisters of the Congregation: secular order, dedicated to teaching children, founded by Marguerite Bourgeoys in 1658.

Sulpicians: priests from the Seminary of Saint-Sulpice in Paris; they arrived in New France in 1657 and became the seigneurs of Montreal in 1663.

Tourtière: a French dish of ground meat in a pie shell

Ursulines: cloistered order of nuns, they arrived in Quebec in 1639 under Marie de l'Incarnation to teach young girls. With them came the Augustinian Hospitalières from Dieppe, France, to work in the Hôtel-Dieu hospital of Quebec.

Voyageur: literally "traveller". Such a man was usually licensed and hired by merchants to cover vast distances by canoe and trade furs with the Natives.

Wampum: a ceremonial Native belt of woven shells; during the fur trade, wampum was made from European glass beads and used as currency.

Resources that were used in writing this book

BOOKS:
There are many books of all levels about New France. Here are a few:

Introduction to New France by Marcel Trudel, (originally in French) (Toronto: Holt, Rinehart and Winston of Canada, 1968)

In the Company of Marguerite Bourgeoys by Sister Florence Quigley (Ottawa: Novalis, 1983)

Life in New France by Jennifer Blizin Gillis, (Picture of the Past series, Chicago: Heinemann Library, 2003)

Jeanne Mance: Foundress of Hôtel-Dieu and Co-Foundress of Montreal (Great Moments in Canadian Church History, Paris: Editions du Rameau). Distributed in Canada by the Jeanne Mance Centre, 251 Pine Avenue West, Montreal.

WEBSITES:

The Virtual Museum of New France
A great website from the Museum of Civilization in Ottawa/Gatineau
http://www.civilization.ca/vmnf/vmnfe.asp

The Early Canadiana Online Collection
A digital library with great links to historical Canadian documents
http://www.canadiana.org/eco/english/collect.html

The First Nations of the New France Era
Provides information about the Six First Nations or aboriginals of Canada
http://collections.ic.gc.ca/premieres_nations/en

New France-New Horizons
A collaboration between France and Canada to create virtual exhibition marking the 400th anniversary of the French presence in North America
http://www.archivescanadafrance.org

Index

Photo and Art Credits

Illustrations by Chrissie Wysotski
Pages 7, 14, 16, 17, 21, 23, 28, 30, 31, 33, 35, 36, 39, 41, 42, 51, 54

Illustrations by Liz Milkau
Cover illustration, page a6

Illustration by Linda Potts
Page 8

Photographs by Joanna Emery
Pages 2, both on page 57

Library and Archives Canada
Pages 4: e002140116, Peter Winkworth Collection of Canadiana R9266-2546, 5: C-005354, 10: C-139973, 18: C-003164, 19: C-010520, Acc. No. 1983-45-1, 20: C-005746, Acc. No. 1990-554-418, 25: C-007885, Acc. No. 1936-239-1, 27: © Library and Archives Canada. Reproduced with the permission of the Minister of Public Works and Government Services Canada (2005). C-005078, Acc No. 1983-45-5, 32: C-009144, 37: C-012340, 38: C-069114, Acc No. 197-6-311, 43: Henri Beau, C-012329, 45: C-089380, Acc. No. 1965-60-28, 48: C-006031, 49: nlc-8722, 52: Henri Beau, C-017059, 53: C-020126, Acc. No. 1996-371-1

Collections des Religieuses Hospitalières de Saint-Joseph
Pages 1, 13, 26, 29, 44

Canada Post
Page 56

Montreal Archives
Page 55